WAKE UP SLEEPING CHURCH

By
Melinda T. Deir-Boyette

All Scripture quotations are taken from the King James Version of the Holy Bible

Copyright © 2022 Melinda Deir-Boyette

All rights reserved.

Library of Congress Control Number: 2022923533

ISBN: 978-1-7347142-0-3 (Paperback)

ISBN: 978-1-7347142-1-0 (eBook)

DEDICATION

This book is dedicated to all seekers
of the Truth and the Light.

> *But seek ye first the kingdom of God, and his righteousness, and all these things shall be added unto you. —Matthews 6:33*

The time has come for the Children of the Living God who are asleep to be awaken. Especially those brainwashed and indoctrinated by false prophets in many institutional churches.

Acknowledgments

I acknowledge my Spiritual Father and Covering,
in Heaven, my Lord and Savior Jesus
Christ of Nazareth, and the Holy Spirit,
who led me to author this book.

Contents

Who Is Your Spiritual Father? 1
The Sleeping Church! 5
Open Our Eyes Lord So We Can See 23
Constructing the Sanctuary 41
Jesus Gives Freedom, Grace and Truth 45
About the Author 51
Other Books by the Author 53

Who Is Your Spiritual Father?

Woe to the rebellious children, saith the Lord, that takes counsel, but not of me; and that cover with a covering, but not of my spirit, that they may add sin to sin.
—Isaiah 30:1

In 2013, my husband and I bought a home in a brand-new subdivision. One of our neighbors tried to befriend my husband. He lived with his wife, a nurse, and he served in the church leadership. Despite my good intentions, I was unable to connect with this neighbor, so I asked my husband not to let him into our house. I was unnerved when he brought an old car and parked it in his driveway. He did not drive the car; it was old, rusted, and leaking oil, causing damage to his driveway and defacing the neighborhood.

To avoid misjudging him, I asked Abba, "Who would buy this nice house and park this old car in his driveway to leak oil?"

VISION OF THE CHURCH LEADER

While sleeping, the Holy Spirit touched my shoulder and said, "Melinda, get up and look through the window." As I looked out the window, I noticed that dozens of people were getting out of the car and heading towards the main road. The Holy Spirit said to me, "The car is a spiritual portal through which those people are going on the main road to cause mischief and accidents. The man is practicing witchcraft."

I shouted, "I see you and I know what you are doing!" My call to him stunned him so much that he quickly turned to look at me up the road. I then stepped out of the vision.

Weeks later, his wife confessed to me that her husband would beat her. In shock, I asked her, "What do you mean your husband beats you?" According to her, he continuously fights with her. As a precaution, I recommended she call the police if he hits her again. In addition, I informed her that she could apply for an immigrant visa as a battered wife under the Immigration and Nationality Act (INA), as amended by the Violence Against Women Act (VAWA); She could apply for her green card without his help if she were taking the abuse out of fear that he will not give her one.

Not long after, I was at my mailbox and the man's wife came over to talk. She told me that her husband had been arrested because she had called the police after he had hit her. She also told me that she had visited her family in Africa. She showed me photographs of her husband smoking marijuana as she ridiculed him for being a church leader, an adulterer, drunkard, and always fighting her.

The Holy Spirit spoke to me as she was talking and told me that her husband was demonized and that when he hit her, he was not seeing her, but seeing a demon, and so he hit her to fight the demon. I was about to tell her that her husband was practicing witchcraft when the Holy Spirit cautioned me not to say anything else. The lady then confirmed that what I told her about her husband being demonized was true, as she had gone to see the witch doctor in her village while she was in Africa, who told her the same thing I had said. According to her, the witch doctor gave her some mojos to keep her safe and secure. Since this woman was also seeking after wizards, I understood why the Holy Spirit told me not to say anything else.

The woman must have told her husband what I had said because not long after that conversation, I was driving home from work, and she stopped me. We exchanged pleasantries at her gate, and when the man saw his wife and me talking, he yelled at me, "Don't talk to my wife! What are you telling her? Do not talk to my wife!" Instead of answering, I drove away. A week later, the wife came to my house and told me her husband had died. I was surprised that he had died, so I inquired what had happened and if he had been sick. According to her, she left him at home well but came home to find him dead on the floor. The Holy Spirit revealed to me that the man was practicing witchcraft and astral projected out of his body and that an angel cut him down. Unfortunately, the lady died in the house four years after her husband's death.

Besides being a church leader, he was an adulterer who abused his wife and practiced witchcraft. How well do you know the person you are calling your church leader, your "spiritual covering" or your "spiritual father"?

> *Then said he unto me, Son of man, hast thou seen what the ancients of the house of Israel do in the dark, every man in the chambers of his imagery? for they say, the Lord seeth us not; the Lord hath forsaken the earth.*
>
> *He said also unto me, Turn thee yet again, and thou shalt see greater abominations that they do. Then he brought me to the door of the gate of the Lord's house which was toward the north; and behold, there sat women weeping for Tammuz.*
>
> *Then said he unto me, Hast thou seen this, O son of man? turn thee yet again, and thou shalt see greater abominations than these.*
> —Ezekiel 8:12:15

The Sleeping Church!

*The hour has already come for you to wake
up from your slumber because our salvation is
nearer now than when we first believed.*
—Romans 13:11

I saw in a vision a Black man winning the presidency of the United States of America while I was in Jamaica during the summer of 2008. "A Black man has won the Presidency for America," I told a friend, who laughed and said, "No, that hasn't happened." Both of us laughed. On November 4, 2008, Barack Obama of Illinois defeated John McCain of Arizona to become the 44th President of the United States.

On June 16, 2015, Donald Trump, the Billionaire Presidential

Candidate, announced his candidacy at Trump Tower in New York City.

Known as the most stunning upset in American history, the billionaire businessman shocked the nation by defeating Hillary Clinton to become the 45th president of the United States. Trump was impeached twice, the only president to be impeached twice in American history.

In 2020, the political atmosphere was charged and most Evangelical Christians championed Trump, calling him "King Cyrus," sent from God to save America. While some loved and idolized him, others hated him, thinking he was reincarnated as "King Herod," sent from the devil.

JOSEPH BIDEN, JR ANNOUNCES HIS CANDIDACY FOR PRESIDENT.

In a video posted on April 25, 2019, Former Vice President Joseph R. Biden, Jr. announced his intention to run for president of the United States in 2020.

Regardless of whom God chooses to rule this great country, I pray for that President in accordance with Romans 13:1. For this reason, when the Holy Spirit prompted me to pray for the Former Vice President Joseph Biden, I was hesitant since all the "major prophets" had predicted Trump would win by a landslide. How could so many prophets be wrong about Trump? One such prophet was a woman I followed on social media and whose ministry I enjoyed. I respected this woman as a "deliverance minister." In addition to pastoring, she also practices medicine. In her ministry videos, I saw people "being delivered." Most of her services revolved around prayer. I wondered, "Is it possible for her to be wrong, God?"

While the deliverance minister claimed prophet status and in her capacity as a physician, this staunch Trump supporter criticized Biden as unfit and demented, saying he could never serve as president because he was demented. As someone who once respected her as a true deliverer and an oracle of God, her behavior appalled and saddened me.

I asked the Lord to please show me this woman, and Abba gave me a vision.

VISION OF THE SLEEPING CHURCH

> *Hear now my words: If there be a prophet among you, I the Lord will make myself known unto him in a vision and will speak unto him in a dream.*
> *—Numbers 12:6*

In my vision, I saw a two-story Mega Ranch church in Texas. In this church, the physician served as the senior pastor. Congregants were seated on the top and bottom floors of the church which was remarkably diverse. As I entered the church, I was dressed in a long yellow flowing dress with a floral pattern, with my hair done in a bob and well groomed.

My attention was drawn to my feet, which were extremely clean, so clean that they glowed. But a shoe was missing. Given my well-dressed appearance in the vision, I was wearing the full armor of God. There was, however, a shoe missing, which indicated that I was missing a shoe of peace. I lost one of my shoes in the vision because all the major prophets that predicted a Trump victory distracted me, and I wavered at the fact that the Holy Spirit told me to pray for Joseph Biden, so I lost my peace.

Let us call the physician/deliverance minister, Ella. As I entered the church, I sat in a corner beside a huge Gothic Wooden Oak Church Door, hoping to be inconspicuous. When Ella realized I was in the church, she scornfully said to her two female armor bearers, "she is clean, she is clean." Ella then shouted at the congregation, "No body talk!" According to Ella, it was forbidden to speak in church. It was as if their bodies were zombies, they only did as they were told and only spoke when spoken to.

After that, Ella turned her back on the congregation and prophesied to one of her armor bearers, telling the armor bearer what she (Ella) already knew about her. As Ella mimed the prophecy, the church was to decipher her words. It occurred to me that what Ella was saying was not a prophecy, but what she already knew. My response was, "That is not a prophecy. How can you tell someone what you know about them and call it a prophecy?" In no way does it constitute a prophecy.

Ella became upset. She came over to me and began shouting at me; she put her hand on my chin to shut my mouth. "You will shut up!" she said, pointing at the Gothic Style Wooden Oak Church Door, "You shall not speak anymore and that will be your grave, and you shall shut up."

I stood up and pointed at Ella and said, "You cannot curse me —I am a child of the Most High God! That shall be your grave and you shall die!" Immediately Ella fell on her back. Suddenly, my eyes opened in the vision, and I saw two visions simultaneously: one spiritual and one natural.

Ella told the first armor bearer to attack me, but she turned into a cloth doll, a huge puppet with the same body size, but she was lightweight. I held her by her feet and started hitting her head on the floor. It was then that I realized I had two angels with me. Although I could not see them, I could hear them clearly, and one said, "You have to smash her head, smash her head." As I focused on Ella, I banged the armor bearer's head on the floor until I was convinced that she had been destroyed.

Ella signaled the second armor bearer to join her in the spiritual realm. Armor bearer two went to Ella in the spirit and kneeled before her in reverence and submission. Ella had a silk blue designer head veil. Wrapped in the head veil as part of her ensnaring techniques was a miniature crystal ball. Ella took out the crystal ball and then screwed off the crown of the armor bearer's head, skull, and all. She then placed the miniature crystal ball inside her head and returned the crown like screwing on a thermos cover. The second armor bearer then turned into a bird. Initially, her spirit was a small fire phoenix, but when she manifested in the natural world, she was a small, scared, naked bird with two little bird feet, but with her normal human face. Note, this is a mega ranch church with ceiling trusses and beams. Armor bearer two flew to the top of the beam which was about fifty feet tall.

My angels were there, so I shouted to one of them, "Hit her down, hit her down!" While I could not see the entire angel's body, I reckoned he was very tall. The angel had a white washrag in his hand and gently tapped the bird. The bird fell, but before it reached the floor, it changed back into the miniature crystal ball Ella had placed in her head. It then occurred to me, "You shall crush your enemy's head, but he will bruise your heels."

As I was in war mode, I shouted to the angel, "You crush it! You crush it, I will not step on it because I do not have my shoe on!" With a huge foot that was about size fifty and brown leather sandals, the angel stepped on the miniature crystal ball, shattering it. A loud pow could be heard as the crystal ball shattered.

This all happened while the entire congregation sat there, mute and doing nothing because Ella had full control over them. They were like zombies after she warned them not to speak. The two armor bearers were destroyed in the church without any words or actions being taken.

As soon as Ella realized her two armor bears had been destroyed, she came over to fight me in the natural world, but she was unable to handle me, so I overpowered her and pinned her to the floor while praying, "God, give me fire so I can cut off her head, just as David cut off Goliath's head and held it up." However, God did not send the fire, so I figured God wanted to spare her life in the vision.

As I was pinning Ella's natural body to the floor, my attention was drawn to a table on the other side of the altar. It was covered with what looked like the communion that Ella planned to give to the people. However, instead of wine, the liquid looked like bleach or a chemical. While I had her pinned to the floor, Ella's spirit got up because she was adamant that she would give the congregation the communion. Ella staggered as she approached the communion table, making me believe that she was exhausted after being beaten.

"Do not drink it! You are sleeping! Wake up!" I shouted. Only five people awoke. I shouted at the few that awoke. "Wake the others! Wake the others! Wake up! You are asleep! Hallelujah is the only way to wake them up! Shout Hallelujah! Shout Hallelujah"! It was silent. No one said a word. They were so afraid of Ella that the ones that woke up did not speak a word.

I left Ella's body on the floor because I decided I was going over to her spirit to fight her, and this time I intended to hurt her. When I looked at Ella's face, to my surprise, she had a blank face in the spirit. There were no ears, no eyes, no mouth, or nose on her. Then I realized why she was staggering; she could not see what was ahead of her. I immediately felt compassion for her when I realized she had lost all her senses in the spiritual realm. Even though Ella was asleep, the members of her congregation who awoke were still afraid of her, whispering to me, "You, wake her, she is asleep, you, wake her, she is asleep."

As a result of Ella not having her senses in the spirit, I was unable to wake her. I arose from the vision.

Often, Ella referred to herself as a spiritual mother with spiritual children. Additionally, she often referred to her church leader as her "spiritual father and covering."

We must never forget the brainwashed Christians, believing that they were following the Bible, "Obey them that have the rule over you." Demonstrating their submission to their Spiritual Father and Spiritual Covering, Pastor Jim Jones and his "spiritual children" partook in the communion of death" in Guyana.

> *But blessed are your eyes, for they see: and your ears, for they hear.* —*Matthew 13:16*

> *Let them alone: they be blind leaders of the blind. And if the blind lead the blind, both shall fall into the ditch.* —Matthew 15:14

> *Woe to the rebellious children, saith the LORD, that takes counsel, but not of me; and that cover with a covering, but not of my spirit, that they may add sin to sin.* —Isaiah 30:1

> *And call no man your father upon the earth: for one is your Father, which is in heaven.*
> —Matthew 23:9

Ella's "deliverance ministry" seemed effective, despite being blind in the Spiritual Realm. The Bible clearly states that false prophets will prophesy in the name of Jesus and that they will perform many miracles and cast out devils in Jesus' name, but in their hearts, they oppose everything Jesus represents.

> *Many will say to me in that day, Lord, Lord, have we not prophesied in thy name? and in thy name have cast out devils? and in thy name done many wonderful works?*
>
> *And then will I profess unto them, I never knew you: depart from me, ye that work iniquity.* —Matthew 7:22-23
>
> *Rejoice not, that the spirits are subject unto you; but rather rejoice, because your names are written in heaven.* —Luke 10:20

> *That at the name of Jesus every knee should bow, of things in heaven, and things in earth, and things under the earth; And that every tongue should confess that Jesus Christ is Lord, to the glory of God the Father.* —Philippians 2:10-11)

THE WHITE HOUSE

A few days after the vision about Ella, I had a vision about Trump being removed from the White House.

The vision was in black and white set during the civil war of 1865, but Donald Trump was president. All the flag poles were covered in mud, and the flags were dirty and tattered. Soldiers were deployed to take down the dirty and torn flags and replace them with new clean ones as others cleaned the mud off the poles.

The Soldiers that brought the new flags and cleaned the poles were ordered to remove President Trump from the White House. After Trump was removed from the Oval Office, all the doors vanished and he was unable to reenter. The vision then changed from black and white display to color. All the flag poles were silver and gleaming, and the flags were flowing in their bright red, white, and blue colors. I arose from the vision.

WARN THE PEOPLE

> *But if the watchman see the sword come, and blow not the trumpet, and the people be not warned; if the sword come, and take any person from among them, he is taken away in his iniquity; but his blood will I require at the watchman's hand. —Ezekiel 33:6*

The Holy Spirit sent me to warn the people that Trump was not going to win the second term. In response to the vision about Ella, Abba led me to Ezekiel 13 which mentions the condemnation of false prophets. In praying for Joseph Biden and warning the people, I felt a peace that I was following God's instructions. In another vision, Abba showed me Georgia and placed a plus sign in Green and the number 1.2 and said, "Watched Georgia." Even though I did not understand what it meant, I continued to pray for Joseph Biden and warned those who would listen not to follow the false prophets who predicted a second term for Trump.

I tried to warn the people that the reason Trump Lost was the cries of those babies and children ripped away from their parents, separated from their lifelines, then locked up in cages, not knowing where their mommies and daddies were. To date some parents cannot be located. —are they alive? Were their bodies buried under the wall?

The children that died in those cages. This went up as a stench to the nostril of God. Although Trump did some good in Israel, what he did to those children and their parents at the border was a cruel atrocity in God's eyes. This is what Abba says. MENE: God has numbered the days of his reign and brought it to an end. TEKEL: he was weighed on the scales and found wanting.

The prophets who prophesied a 2020 Trump win prophesied their desires. *2 Thessalonians 2:11* And for this cause God shall send them strong delusion, that they should believe a lie: Lying Prophets —*Ezekiel 13*

GOD HAS SPOKEN, and he has chosen Joseph R. Biden as the 46th President of the United States of America. I am just the messenger, the least in the Kingdom, but yes Abba does give me messages to deliver at times. No, God did not smite President Obama/Biden for building those cages; as you know, God made President Obama a two-term president. Yes, President Obama built the cages, as "a 72-hour holding location for BOTH parents and children, who were "the undocumented immigrants." Trump separated those children—who were as young as a couple of months old—from their parents and locked up those babies! Do you know who else separated children from their parents? A wicked king named Herod, and do you know who was an undocumented immigrant? A man called Jesus Christ of Nazareth, The Messiah, and his parents.

> *It were better for him that a millstone were hanged about his neck, and he cast into the sea, than that he should offend one of these little ones. —Luke 17:2*

> *And when they were departed, behold, the angel of the Lord appeareth to Joseph in a dream, saying, Arise, and take the young child and his mother, and flee into Egypt, and be thou there until I bring thee word: for Herod will seek the young child to destroy him. —Matthew 2:13*

LED TO PRAY

> *Also, seek the peace and prosperity of the city to which I have carried you into exile. Pray to the LORD for it, because if it prospers, you too will prosper* —Jeremiah 29:7

On social media pages set up to support Joseph Biden, I recorded my prayers for the candidate:

"Holy Father. To lead the Great United States of America, I pray Abba that you gives Joseph Biden wisdom greater than Solomon's. Righteous Father, you change times and seasons. You depose kings and raise others."

"You give wisdom to the wise and knowledge to the discerning. Our heavenly Father's wisdom is first pure, then peaceful, gentle, open to reason, full of mercy and good fruits, and impartial and sincere. The harvest of righteousness is sown in peace by those who make peace."

"Abba, I pray Joseph Biden keeps his eyes on you and always seeks you for guidance. Righteous Father, please lead Joseph to the White House as you led Joseph of the Bible to be the second most powerful ruler of Egypt, endowed with great visions, knowledge and understanding. Bless whatever he puts his hands to. I pray Abba that you make Joseph Biden great in all the world and give him great peace of mind, and like Hezekiah, Holy Father, please give Joe Health and extend his life. Also, Righteous Father, please bless his precious wife and family, our nation, and your people. I thank you Abba, for this I pray in the mighty name of Jesus Christ of Nazareth. Amen."

THE VICIOUS CHRISTIANS

As a "Christian," I am stunned when Christians who follow Trump and idolize him become enraged and vicious towards other Christians who do not share their ideals. The "Christians, evangelicals" who support Trump have verbally attacked, unfriended, and blocked me on social media, because they said Trump is God's choice and by supporting and voting for Biden, I am ushering in the "New World Order." When I said Trump would not be re-elected in 2020, they called me a witch, Jezebel, and everything else but a child of God. I could not believe how engrossed Christians were in the election—it was as if America were under a spell. According to them, they would not listen to me because their prophets heard from God and they believed these prophets that God sent to them. Some quote the Bible verse 2 Chronicles 20:20.

> *"Believe in the LORD your God, so shall ye be established; believe his prophets, so shall ye prosper." —2 Chronicles 20:20*

Despite this, I continued to warn everyone who would listen of the dangers of being overly emotional when Trump lost.

There were a few who were responsive, and a few apologized for treating me harshly.

After three days of counting in a long and bitter election, Democrat Joseph Biden was elected to be the 46th president of the United States of America. Many evangelicals who prophesied a landslide victory that would give President Trump a second term did not repent when Trump lost, instead they doubled down and gave more prophecies and refused to repent. There were a few repentances, but most remained unrepentant. They did not get their lesson in humility.

THAT WILL NEVER HAPPEN IN AMERICA
"There will be chaos in congress on January 6, 2021," I told my husband the day before the counting of the 2020 electoral votes. To my husband, it was unfathomable to think that such an event could happen in The United States of America, Washington DC, and even more so, that it could take place on the Capitol Grounds or in the Capitol building. He confidently replied, "Honey, things like that will never happen in America."

Donald Trump and his supporters refused to concede the 2020 presidential election. Pro-Trump rioters stormed the United States Capitol building on January 6, 2021, after gathering on the Ellipse of the Capitol complex for a rally entitled "Save America March." Despite the violence, death toll and injuries, Vice President Mike Pence declared President-Elect

Joseph Biden, Jr. the winner of the presidential election after Congress finally counted the electoral votes.

FALSE PROPHETS

Those who predicted Trump would win a second term are the same ones who predicted a Red Wave in 2022. Again, the people believe the lies.

> "The prophets prophesy lies, the priests rule by their authority, and my people love it this way. But what will you do in the end?" — *Jeremiah 5:31*

> "You have profaned me among my people for a few handfuls of barley and scraps of bread. By lying to my people, who listen to lies."
> —*Ezekiel 13:19*

According to some of the false prophets, God promised a second term to Trump, but their prophecies did not happen. Once again, they predicted a Red Wave in the 2022 midterms, and those who followed them believed their lies. The red waves did not occur. Though Republicans took the House with a narrow majority, they underperformed. Compared to Former President Donald Trump, President Joseph Biden had a great night in the 2022 midterms.

The Democratic Party had forty-eight senators when President-elect Biden won the election in November 2020. Two years later, following the 2022 Midterm Election, Democrats hold 51 Senate seats, defying historical polls and expectations.

On November 15, 2022, Trump announced his third bid for the presidency.

We will have to wait and see what the prophets and evangelicals have to say about Former President Trump's presidency in 2024. Are they going to prophesy lies for some barley and scraps of bread, or will they follow Jesus Christ of Nazareth and be the Church, the body of Christ? Regardless of whom God chooses to rule this great nation, let us pray for that person according to Romans 13:1.

> *"Let everyone be subject to the governing authorities, for there is no authority except that which God has established. The authorities that exist have been established by God."*
> *— Romans 13:1*

Open Our Eyes Lord So We Can See

*They said unto him, Lord, that our eyes
may be opened. —Matthew 20:33*

In the Mighty name of Jesus Christ of Nazareth and through his precious blood, I believe God assigned me to help my brothers and sisters in Christ Jesus who are asleep and in bondage to be awakened, delivered, and set free.

Recently, I felt God leading me to a pastor's social media page. Having not received any explicit instructions from Abba about why I should visit the website, I went with an open mind. I was attentively listening and participating in the sermon, adding emojis to show my agreement and saying "amen" until the sermon turned from preaching the word to condemning for not paying tithes, and questioning people's integrity for not paying tithes.

To remain respectful and humble, I politely said, "I have read the Bible and I always see tithing connected to agriculture and livestock." This irritated the pastor, but she stayed calm. As she continued, "Truth lives here, and if you don't agree with my theology, you can visit many other churches."

"I must be missing something," I thought. Because I cannot fathom how so many resolute pastors preach that people should pay a tithe and that a God who sacrificed his son for us will curse those who receive him if they fail to pay ten percent of all their earnings, then to be badgered and have their integrity questioned if they do not pay their pastor ten percent on a weekly basis. Those pastors are the ones that need an integrity check.

The pastor continued to say that truth lives within her, that we are no longer farmers and that we live in a first-world country, so we cannot continue to give animals. The pastor repeated that we do not sell cows or chickens, we cannot fill the temple with chickens, and we do not raise pigs. She state that since money was not available in those days, agricultural products and livestock were exchanged by bartering rather than paying with money.

The pastor even mentioned that stone was used as currency in the past. I was surprised that she had no idea money existed before God gave Moses the laws. She is part of the sleeping Church. According to the Holy Bible, money was around even before Moses was born. Is there any reason a pastor would not know that? Does she deliriously lie to her church members? Does she intentionally deceive or lie to her church members? Or is she sleeping?

I prayed and wept for her, asking God to open her eyes. At best, she is asleep and needs to wake up. I did not know what to believe about her after this. How could a pastor be unaware that money existed before Moses?

In response to the pastor's comment, "we no longer bring cows, chickens, or pigs to church." One of her congregants mockingly wrote, "Pastor, I'm bringing a goat to church on Sunday." Their delusion was evident to me.

People who claim God commanded tithes to be agricultural products because money did not exist at that time are not speaking the truth. When the Truth is distorted, I must speak out as a seeker of the Truth. In the search for truth and light, I seek to know the truth.

Like Ella, this pastor's "spiritual father," her spiritual covering is not the Lord Jesus Christ of Nazareth and her covering is not the Holy Spirit. I sensed that this pastor was blind in the Spirit and believing her truth, so God sent her a strong delusion.

> *For this reason, God sends them a powerful delusion so that they will believe the lie.*
> —*2 Thessalonians 2:11*

THE HOLY SPIRIT LEADS IN ALL TRUTH

It is important to keep in mind that whenever God says money, he means money, and when he says agricultural products, he means agricultural products. This relates to the law of tithing, freewill offering and giving money exclusively to the temple.

Those who gained their income from the sea or things they made with their hands did not have to give tithes, since the Law of Moses only required Israelite farmers and herders to pay tithes on their increase. Gentiles, fishermen, carpenters, priests, and merchandisers did not have to tithe.

> *And concerning the tithe of the herd, or of the flock, even of whatsoever passeth under the rod, the tenth shall be holy unto the Lord.*
> —*Leviticus 27:32*

According to the Law (or Old Covenant), tithing came from agricultural products.

"You shall truly tithe all the increase of your grain that the field produces year by year. And you shall eat before the Lord your God, in the place where He chooses to make His name abide, the tithe of your grain and your new wine and your oil, of the firstborn of your herds and your flocks, that you may learn to fear the Lord your God always. But if the journey is too long for you so that you are not able to carry the tithe, or if the place where the Lord your God chooses to put His name is too far from you when the Lord your God has blessed you, then you shall exchange it for MONEY, take the MONEY in your hand, and go to the place which the Lord your God chooses. And you shall spend that money for whatever your heart desires: for oxen or sheep, for wine or similar drink, for whatever your heart desires; you shall eat there before the Lord your God, and you shall rejoice, you and your household. You shall not forsake the Levite who is within your gates, for he has no part nor inheritance with you. —Deuteronomy 14:22-27

DO NO HARM

> And many shall follow their pernicious ways; by reason of whom the way of truth shall be evil spoken of. And through covetousness shall they with feigned words make merchandise of you: whose judgment now of a long time lingereth not, and their damnation slumbereth not.
> —2 Peter 2:3

To ensnare, manipulate and swindle their congregations for their money and possessions, wolves disguised as shepherds have twisted and used the following stories:

THE COIN IN THE FISH'S MOUTH

Jesus Christ of Nazareth is the true Temple, and he is the truth and the light, no lie can be found in him, so when Peter lied to the temple door collector, Jesus had to make it right. While Jesus went to the Temple several times throughout his life, he never paid a temple tax, the bible even tells of Jesus overturning the money in the Temple. However, to correct Peter's lie since Jesus is the Truth. Jesus sent Peter to get the money from the fish's mouth, not to endorse tithing, but to demonstrate his integrity and not to cause an offense.

> *And when they were come to Capernaum, they that received tribute money came to Peter, and said, Doth not your master pay tribute? He saith, Yes. And when he was come into the house, Jesus prevented him, saying, What thinkest thou, Simon? of whom do the kings of the earth take custom or tribute? of their own children, or of strangers? Peter saith unto him, Of strangers. Jesus saith unto him, Then are the children free. Notwithstanding, lest we should offend them, go thou to the sea, and cast an hook, and take up the fish that first cometh up; and when thou hast opened his mouth, thou shalt find a piece of money: that take, and give unto them for me and thee. —Matthew 17:24-27*

REMEMBER MERCY, JUDGEMENT AND FAITH

Jesus in Luke 11 did not endorse the tithe. Jesus was encouraging the Pharisees to continue in the law but to practice the most important law which is love. Jesus was not yet crucified, his precious blood was not yet ransomed for our sins, and the law was not yet fulfilled. Again, the tithe Jesus was speaking about was the agricultural products and specifically the Pharisees Garden herbs.

> *But woe unto you, Pharisees! for ye tithe mint and rue and all manner of herbs and pass over judgment and the love of God: these ought ye to have done, and not to leave the other undone.*
> *—Luke 11:42*

ANANIAS AND SAPPHIRA

It is common for pastors and apostles to use the story of Ananias and Sapphira to scare their members into giving them money, but if we examine the story closely, we discover that Peter and the Apostles were not preaching the true Gospel.

Despite his status as the head of the Jewish Church, Peter had flaws as well. In addition to performing miracles, signs, and wonders, Peter was also leading the church astray, practicing racism, hate, and not preaching the truth of the Gospel. (Galatians 2:11-14)

Peter displays leadership qualities when he steps forward to represent the Twelve when Jesus asks, "But who say you that I am? Jesus told Peter that the Church would be built on him.

> *And I say also unto thee, That thou art Peter, and upon this rock, I will build my church; and the gates of hell shall not prevail against it.*
> *—Matthew 16:18*

The enemy of our souls, however, was not going to make it easy for Peter to lead the church. In response to Satan's request, Peter was sifted as wheat.

> And the Lord said, Simon, Simon, behold, Satan hath desired to have you, that he may sift you as wheat. But I have prayed for thee, that thy faith fail not: **and when thou art converted, strengthen thy brethren.** —Luke 22:31-32

In Matthew 14:22-33, Peter lost faith and sank when walking on water toward Jesus; in John 18:15-2, Peter denies knowing Christ three times.

Peter was reinstated by Jesus and commissioned to feed His sheep. Three times Jesus encouraged him to care for His flock—John 21:15-16. Peter's ministry should epitomize restoration and grace, yet Ananias and Sapphira did not receive that patience, grace, love, and restoration from Peter.

> ...behold, the feet of them which have buried thy husband are at the door, and shall carry thee out. Then fell she down straightway at his feet, and yielded up the ghost: and the young men came in, and found her dead, and, carrying her forth, buried her by her husband. And great fear came upon all the church, and upon as many as heard these things. —Acts 5:9-11

Peter fell again and was not walking in love through the blood of Jesus Christ and the truth of the gospel, Satan must have returned to sift Peter again. (Luke 4:13).

Peter refused to allow the Holy Spirit to lead him for a time. Although Jesus told him and the other disciples that no one could predict when he would return because the Father fixed that time by his authority (Acts 1:7). Peter convinced his congregation that they would see Jesus' return, so they sold their properties and gave all their money to the apostles.

Peter was the leader of the early church and the people revered him as their Apostle and leader. He was their "Spiritual Father and Spiritual Covering." They witnessed the miracles, signs, and wonders he performed. They knew he and his brother Apostle Andrew were the first dis-ciples to walk with Jesus Christ and were in Jesus' inner circle with James and John. Peter quit his business to follow Jesus.

In the minds of his followers, there was no reason for Peter to be unaware of the return of Jesus to earth. Peter's followers believed the Apostles to their demise, as well as the deaths of Ananias and Sapphira.

The Spirit of God does not instill fear in us but love, power, and a sound mind. Therefore, what spirit caused the great fear that fell on the Church of the Living God? Fear killed Ananias and Sapharria, not God.

The Holy Spirit did not lead Peter's audience; they followed the Apostles and walked in fear, losing their power and sound minds. According to the Bible, they were in great fear, and common sense tells us they were mentally unstable since they sold all their possessions and gave them away because a man told them to. They sold their properties and quit their jobs. Two thousand years have passed and Jesus Christ has still not returned.

Paul told us not to sell our properties, but that each person should work and live quiet lives.

> *And that ye study to be quiet, and to do your own business, and to work with your own hands, as we commanded you; That ye may walk honestly toward them that are without, and that ye may have lack of nothing.*
> *—1 Thessalonians 4:11-12*

The apostle Peter said that Ananias and Sapphira lied to the Holy Spirit and consequently, they died. How could they have lied to the Holy Spirit when Peter was not preaching the truth of the Gospel or being led by the Holy Spirit? Peter was working miracles, signs, and wonders but he stood condemned. Jesus while he walked the earth as God in the flesh told the disciples not to get excited when demons are subject to them (Luke 10:20)

> *...rejoice not, that the spirits are subject unto you; but rather rejoice, because your names are written in heaven. —Luke 10:20*

If Peter had not encouraged people to sell their property, this would never have happened. Peter caused great fear to fall upon God's church, and Peter himself fell into fear as a result. Jesus told Peter, "For all who take the sword shall perish with the sword." (Matthew 26:52)

Jesus Christ of Nazareth told his disciples that the gospel would be preached throughout the world, and when that is accomplished, the end will come. (Matthew 24:14). Jesus again reminded his disciples to go into the world and preach the gospel to everyone. (Mark 16:15)

> *But when Peter was come to Antioch, I withstood him to the face, because he was to be blamed. For before that certain came from James, he did eat with the Gentiles: but when they were come, he withdrew and separated himself, fearing them which were of the circumcision. And the other Jews dissembled likewise with him; insomuch that **Barnabas also was carried away with their dissimulation**. But when I saw that **they walked not uprightly according to the truth of the gospel**, I said unto Peter before them all, If thou, being a Jew, livest after the manner of Gentiles, and not as do the Jews, why compellest thou the Gentiles to live as do the Jews? —Galatians 2:11-14*

Peter forgot all Jesus had said, he excluded Gentiles and advised Jews to sell their properties because Jesus would return within their lifetimes or much sooner. After Paul confronted and rebuked him, Peter repented and returned to preaching the truth according to the Gospel of Jesus Christ of Nazareth. Peter broke through the walls of segregation and walked in love, acceptance, and patience. (2 Peter 3:15-18).

And account that the longsuffering of our Lord is salvation; even as our beloved brother Paul also according to the wisdom given unto him hath written unto you; As also in all his epistles, speaking in them of these things; in which are some things hard to be understood, which they that are unlearned and unstable wrest, as they do also the other scriptures, unto their own destruction.

Ye therefore, beloved, seeing ye know these things before, beware lest ye also, being led away with the error of the wicked, fall from your own steadfastness. But grow in grace, and in the knowledge of our Lord and Saviour Jesus Christ. To him be glory both now and forever. Amen.
—2 Peter 3:15-18

And this gospel of the kingdom shall be preached in all the world for a witness unto all nations; and then shall the end come. —Matthew 24:14

> *And he said unto them, Go ye into all the world, and preach the gospel to every creature. - Mark 16:15)*

Who are your spiritual parents and what are they teaching? Despite the miracles, signs, and wonders they perform, are they leading you astray? Glory to God the Apostle Peter repented after Apostle Paul confronted him.

WE ARE NOW UNDER A NEW COVENANT WITH JESUS CHRIST OUR GREAT HIGH PRIEST

> *For when the priesthood is changed, the law must be changed also.* —Hebrews 7:12

Melchizedek received ten percent of Abram's spoils of war, but Abram gave ninety percent to the wicked king of Sodom. Abraham never tithe from his personal wealth or possessions.

> *Then Melchizedek king of Salem brought out bread and wine. He was the priest of God Most High, and he blessed Abram, saying, "Blessed be Abram by God Most High, Creator of heaven and earth. And praise be to God Most High, who delivered your enemies into your hand" Then Abram gave him a tenth of everything.*
>
> *The king of Sodom said to Abram, "Give me the people and keep the goods for yourself. "But Abram said to the king of Sodom, "With the raised hand I have sworn an oath to the Lord, God Most High, Creator of heaven and earth, that I will accept nothing belonging to you, not even a thread or the strap of a sandal so that you will never be able to say, 'I made Abram rich.' I will accept nothing but what my men have eaten and the share that belongs to the men who went with me—to Aner, Eshkol, and Mamre. Let them have their share."*
> *—Genesis 31:41*

SAY YES OR NO

> *Say only 'yes' if you mean 'yes,' and say only 'no' if you mean 'no.' If you say more than that, it is from the Evil One.* —Matthew 5:37

Jacob vowed to tithe and make a deal with God that he would tithe only if God granted him everything he requested.

> *And Jacob vowed a vow, saying, If God will be with me, and will keep me in this way that I go, and will give me bread to eat, and raiment to put on, So that I come again to my father's house in peace; then shall the Lord be my God: And this stone, which I have set for a pillar, shall be God's house: and of all that thou shalt give me I will surely give the tenth unto thee.*
> —Genesis 28:20-22

It is not referenced in the Bible that Jacob tithed and the Bible clearly says that Jacob did not return to his father's house until decades later. We know that Jacob worked for his uncle for at least 20 years and did not return to his father's house soon after.

For 20 years, Jacob worked under difficult conditions with Laban, caring for his livestock and animals.

> *Thus, have I been twenty years in thy house; I served thee fourteen years for thy two daughters, and six years for thy cattle: and thou hast changed my wages ten times. —Genesis 31:41*

Constructing the Sanctuary

As part of the instructions that God gave Moses for the Temple, he collected money that would be used exclusively for the Temple. The claim that money did not exist when God gave Moses the Law of tithing is malicious because, in addition God gave Moses instruction to collect money from the Israelites and use the money exclusively for constructing, maintaining and for the Temple business.

> *Everyone that passeth among them that are numbered, from twenty years old and above, shall give an offering unto the Lord. The rich shall not give more, and the poor shall not give less than half a shekel, when they give an offering unto the Lord, to make an atonement for your souls. And thou shalt take the atonement money of the children of Israel, and shalt appoint it for the service of the tabernacle of the congregation; that it may be a memorial unto the children of Israel before the Lord, to make an atonement for your souls.*
> —Exodus 30:11-16

King Josiah did what was right in God's eyes and throughout his reign, he followed the ways of his father David. Josiah repaired the Lord's House using money and without manipulating the people.

Go up to Hilkiah the high priest, that he may sum the silver which is brought into the house of the Lord, which the keepers of the door have gathered of the people: And let them deliver it into the hand of the doers of the work, that have the oversight of the house of the Lord: and let them give it to the doers of the work which is in the house of the Lord, to repair the breaches of the house, Unto carpenters, and builders, and masons, and to buy timber and hewn stone to repair the house.

Howbeit there was no reckoning made with them of the money that was delivered into their hand, because they dealt faithfully. And Hilkiah the high priest said unto Shaphan the scribe, I have found the book of the law in the house of the Lord. And Hilkiah gave the book to Shaphan, and he read it. And Shaphan the scribe came to the king, and brought the king word again, and said, Thy servants have gathered the money that was found in the house and have delivered it into the hand of them that do the work, that have the oversight of the house of the Lord.
—2 Kings 22:4-9

Jesus Gives Freedom, Grace and Truth

Stand fast therefore in the liberty wherewith Christ hath made us free and be not entangled again with the yoke of bondage. —Galatians 5:1

An example of free-will giving: the New Testament cites Cornelius praying and giving money to the poor.

> *Cornelius, thy prayer is heard, and thine alms are in remembrance in the sight of God.*
> *—Acts 10:31*

The centurion built the Synagogue for God's people with his money.

> *For he loveth our nation, and he hath built us a synagogue.* —Luke 7:4-5

Additionally, some women gave their money to Jesus Christ when he walked the earth as God in the flesh.

> *And certain women, which had been healed of evil spirits and infirmities, Mary called Magdalene, out of whom went seven devils, And Joanna the wife of Chuza Herod's steward, and Susanna, and many others, which ministered unto him of their substance.* —Luke 8:2-3

> *And there came a certain poor widow, and she threw in two mites, which make a farthing. And he called unto him his disciples, and saith unto them, Verily I say unto you, That this poor widow hath cast more in, than all they which have cast into the treasury: For all, they did cast in of their abundance; but she of her want did cast in all that she had, even all her living.* — Mark 12:42-44

The Apostle Paul teaches us how to give and shows us in the Bible how a true Apostle loves and cares for his congregations.

> *Behold, the third time I am ready to come to you; and I will not be burdensome to you: for I seek not yours, but you: for the children ought not to lay up for the parents, but the parents for the children.* —2 Corinthians 12:14

> *Upon the first day of the week let every one of you lay by him in store, as God hath prospered him, that there be no gatherings when I come.* - 1 Corinthians 16:2

> *But this I say, He which soweth sparingly shall reap also sparingly; and he which soweth bountifully shall reap also bountifully. Every man according as he purposeth in his heart, so let him give; not grudgingly, or of necessity: for God loveth a cheerful giver.* —2 Corinthians 9:6-7

The Bible clearly says that there was money when Christ walked the earth. The Old Testament first mentions money in Genesis when Abraham buys a burial plot for his wife Sarah.

> *And Abraham hearkened unto Ephron; and Abraham weighed to Ephron the silver, which he had named in the audience of the sons of Heth, four hundred shekels of silver, current money with the merchant. —Genesis 23:16*

I pray that people's eyes will be opened to this truth. No one can change God's laws.

God is the Supreme Judge of the Universe; he is the Supreme Ruler. When the Supreme God rules on a constitutional Law, that judgment is final; only God can alter this decision. Through the precious blood of Jesus Christ of Nazareth, Abba amended the old Laws.

> *God the Supreme Ruler, God standeth in the congregation of the mighty; he judgeth among the gods. —Psalm 82:1*

> *For the preaching of the cross is to them that perish foolishness; but unto us which are saved it is the power of God. —1 Corinthians 1:18*

About the Author

Best-selling and award-winning author, the Jamaican-born Melinda Deir-Boyette is first a wife and mother who considers it her privilege to share the good news about how Christ saves and loves all his children. Her sense of humor and biblical background enables her to share her knowledge with believers and unbelievers. A minister of the Lord Jesus Christ of Nazareth, her goal is to go into the world, heal the sick, raise the dead, and set captives free, especially Christians who have been taught lies in institutional churches.

Other Books by the Author

JESUS CHRIST IS REAL
King of Kings and Lord of Lords

A Memoir of Love
By
Melinda T. Deir-Boyette

Library of Congress Control Number: 2020900219
ISBN 978-0-578-63168-4 (paperback)
ISBN 978-1-7347142-3-4 (audio)
ISBN 978-1-7347142-6-5 (eBook)

Visit: www.deirtodream.com

www.ingramcontent.com/pod-product-compliance
Lightning Source LLC
Chambersburg PA
CBHW061731070526
44583CB00024B/3099